Add to your Maths skills with CGP!

This fantastic CGP book is exactly what pupils need to become champions of Year 5 Addition and Subtraction.

It's crammed full of quick-fire tests — each one takes 10 minutes. They get tougher through the book, building up the skills to take on adding and subtracting questions of all difficulties.

To top it off, we've included full answers to every question — plus a handy chart to check progress too!

What CGP is all about

Our sole aim here at CGP is to produce the highest quality books — carefully written, immaculately presented and dangerously close to being funny.

Then we work our socks off to get them out to you — at the cheapest possible prices.

Published by CGP

Editors: Sean McParland and Ben Train

With thanks to Glenn Rogers and Emma Wright for the proofreading.

With thanks to Jan Greenway for the copyright research.

ISBN: 978 1 78908 646 1

Clipart from Corel®
Printed by Elanders Ltd, Newcastle upon Tyne.

Based on the classic CGP style created by Richard Parsons.

Contents

How to Use this Book

- This book contains <u>12 tests</u>, all geared towards improving your addition and subtraction skills.

- Each test is out of <u>11 marks</u> and should take about <u>10 minutes</u> to complete.

- Each test starts with some <u>warm-up questions</u> to get you going and ends with a <u>problem-solving question</u>.

- The tests <u>increase in difficulty</u> as you go through the book.

- <u>Answers</u> and a <u>Progress Chart</u> can be found at the <u>back</u> of the book.

Warm up

1.　Work out the answers to these calculations in your head.

　　a)　2331 + 8 = ...　　　b)　5078 + 4 = ...　　<u>　　　　</u>
　　1 mark

2.　Work out the answers to these calculations in your head.

　　a)　9422 – 6000 = ...　　b)　4806 – 300 = ...

　　c)　3715 – 2000 = ...　　d)　7689 – 500 = ...　<u>　　　　</u>
　　2 marks

3.　Work out the answers to these calculations.

```
    8  2  1  0            5  3  1  5
+   1  5  8  2        +   3  1  4  2
-----------           -----------

.................     .................
```

<u>　　　　</u>
2 marks

4.　Draw lines to connect each calculation to the inverse that could be used to check the answer.

| 54 + 18 = 72 | 54 – 18 = 36 | 154 – 118 = 36 |

| 36 + 118 = 154 | 72 – 18 = 54 | 36 + 18 = 54 |

<u>　　　　</u>
2 marks

5. Work out the answers to these calculations.

        7 . 3 9   9 . 7 3
      − 3 . 2 6   − 4 . 4 1
      ‾‾‾‾‾‾‾‾‾   ‾‾‾‾‾‾‾‾‾

      ....
      ‾‾‾‾‾‾‾‾‾   ‾‾‾‾‾‾‾‾‾

                                                                    ‾‾‾‾‾‾‾
                                                                    2 marks

6. Tessa goes to the supermarket to buy apples and broccoli.
The supermarket's price list is shown below.

Apples	£1.75
Peppers	£2.20
Broccoli	£2.15
Lemons	£1.25

Tessa pays with a £10 note. How much change will she get?

                                                    £ ....   ‾‾‾‾‾‾‾
                                                                                 2 marks

END OF TEST

/ 11

Warm up

1. Work out the answers to these calculations in your head.

   a) 3784 – 3 = ...   b) 8049 – 6 = ...

   1 mark

2. Work out the answers to these calculations in your head.

   a) 2618 + 60 = ...   b) 9225 + 30 = ...

   c) 8061 + 50 = ...   d) 3384 + 40 = ...

   2 marks

3. Work out:

   4738 + 1411

   ....   _1 mark_

   6835 + 914

   ....   _1 mark_

4. Work out the answers to these calculations.

   ```
     7 2 5 7          6 4 2 6
   – 4 2 1 4        – 5 2 1 1
   ─────────        ─────────

   .............      .............
   ```

   2 marks

5. Work out:

5.52 − 2.47

....
1 mark

9.8 − 2.23

....
1 mark

6. Rhodri has five number cards:

| 1236 | 1436 | 1886 |

| 250 | 400 |

He adds together a white card and a grey card.
He then subtracts a white card from a grey card.
His two answers are the same. He uses each card only once.

Which number does Rhodri **not** use in his two calculations?

....
2 marks

END OF TEST

/ 11

Test 2

Warm up

1. Fill in the gaps to complete these calculations.

   a) 3158 – .... = 3152

   b) 8245 – .... = 8225

   c) .... – 40 = 1851

   d) .... – 6 = 4039

   2 marks

2. Circle **both** of the inverse calculations that you could use to check the answer to 45 + 68 = 113.

   113 – 45   68 – 45   45 + 68 + 113   113 – 68

   1 mark

3. Work out:

   9219 + 4203   3775 + 1869

   ....

   2 marks

4. A factory makes cars that are either red or blue.
   It makes 2150 cars on Monday and 1650 cars on Tuesday.

   If 2320 of the cars were red, how many of the cars were blue?

   .... cars

   2 marks

5. Work out:

6589 – 5836

.... $\overline{\text{1 mark}}$

9956 – 448

.... $\overline{\text{1 mark}}$

6. Parvati has written some numbers on rectangular pieces of paper. She arranges them so that each number is equal to the sum of the two numbers below it.

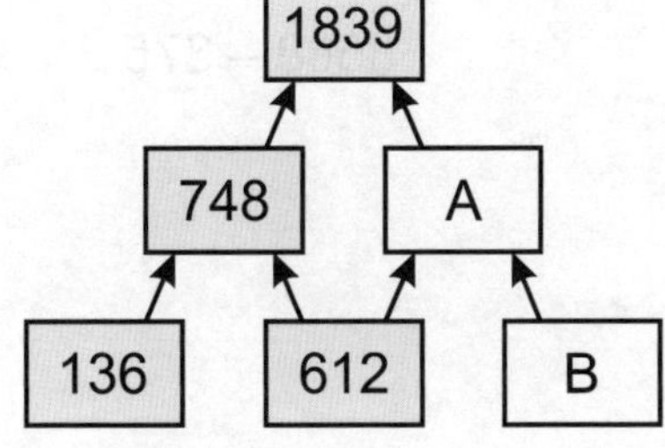

What numbers should go in rectangles A and B?

A: ....

B: .... $\overline{\text{2 marks}}$

END OF TEST

/ 11

Warm up

1. Work out the answers to these calculations in your head.

    a) 2971 – 600 = ...

    b) 1682 – 40 = ...

    c) 4203 – 30 = ...

    d) 8034 – 700 = ...
    ____
    2 marks

2. Fill in the blanks to complete these calculations.

    a) 2548 + ... = 2748

    b) 9115 + ... = 9145
    ____
    1 mark

3. Work out:

    8717 – 2912   3568 – 375

    ....
    ____
    2 marks

4. Circle the best estimate for each of these calculations.

    | 512 + 294 | 600 | 700 | 800 | 900 |

    | 3201 – 1933 | 0 | 1000 | 2000 | 3000 |
    ____
    2 marks

5. Work out the answers to these calculations.

```
  6 . 6 2              5 . 3 4
+ 2 . 4 5            + 3 . 2 9
─────────            ─────────
................      ................
```

2 marks

6. David put the items below into his empty backpack.

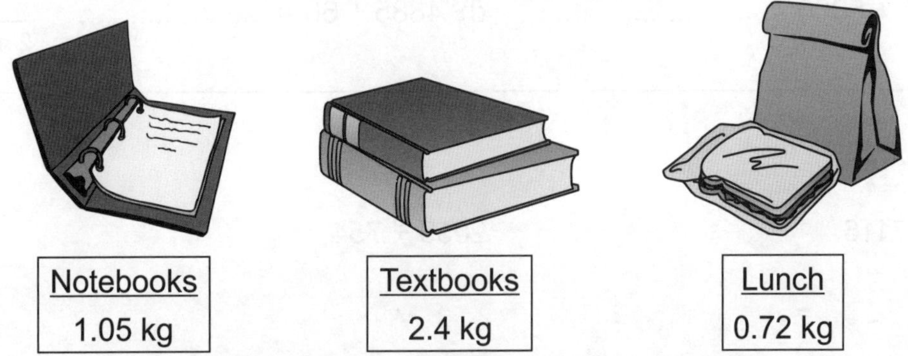

His backpack weighed 4.95 kg once he had put everything inside.

How much did his backpack weigh when it was empty?

.... kg

2 marks

END OF TEST

/ 11

(10)

Warm up

1. Circle **both** of the inverse calculations that you
   could use to check the answer to 578 − 394 = 184.

   578 + 184   184 + 394   184 − 394   578 − 184

   1 mark

2. Work out the answers to these calculations in your head.

   a) 8792 + 300 = ...   b) 1057 + 7 = ...

   c) 3491 + 5000 = ...   d) 4885 + 60 = ...

   2 marks

3. Work out:

   9644 + 7116   2059 + 754

   ....

   2 marks

4. A café opens a box of 1040 tea bags on Monday.
   They use 412 of the tea bags on Monday and 395 on Tuesday.

   How many tea bags does the café have left to use on Wednesday?

   .... tea bags

   2 marks

5. Work out the answers to these calculations.

```
    8 . 2  3              5 . 1  2
  - 4 . 0  5            - 2 . 8  0
  ___________           ___________

  ...............        ...............
  ___________           ___________
```

2 marks

6. Three runners competed in a race.
The scoreboard below shows one of their times.

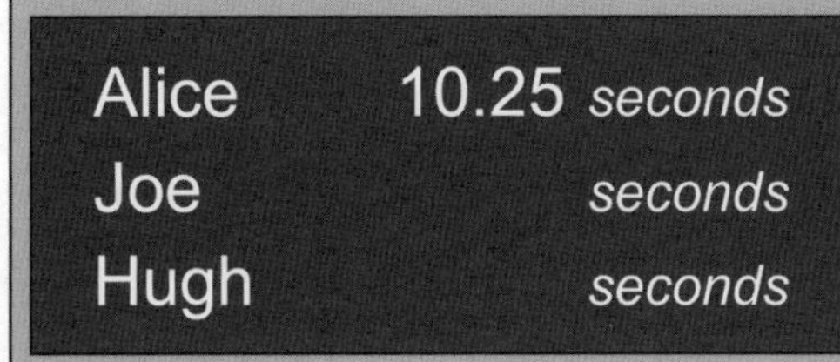

Joe was 2.44 seconds slower than Alice.
Hugh was 1.72 seconds faster than Joe.

What was Hugh's time?

.... seconds

2 marks

END OF TEST

/ 11

Warm up

1. Work out the answers to these calculations in your head.

   a) 516 + 199 = ... b) 267 + 401 = ...

   c) 455 + 203 = ... d) 738 + 96 = ...

   2 marks

2. Work out the answers to these calculations in your head.

   a) 503 − 299 = ... b) 986 − 501 = ...

   1 mark

3. Work out:

   9702 − 2866   6261 − 819

   ....

   2 marks

4. Draw lines to connect each calculation to its best estimate.

   | 924 − 189 | | 321 + 287 | | 694 + 113 |

   | 600 | | 700 | | 800 |

   2 marks

5. Work out:

    9.33 – 3.79   4.24 – 2.67

....   __________

                                                              2 marks

6. Li is playing a game. She has to get her
    playing piece from the start to the finish line.

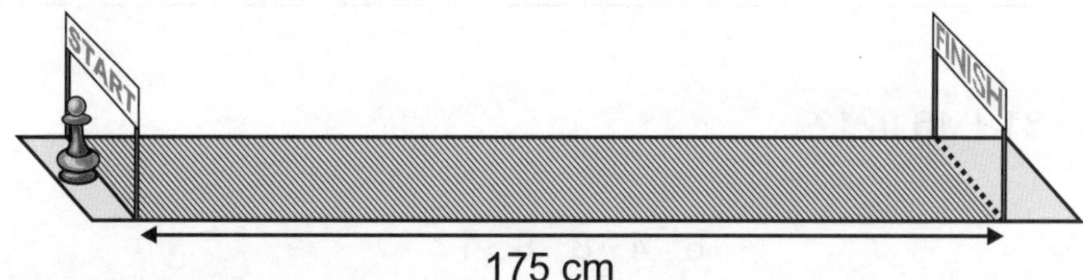

It moves 81 cm forwards, 33 cm backwards
and then 75 cm forwards.

How far is the piece from the finish line?

                                               .... cm   __________

                                                              2 marks

END OF TEST

/ 11

Warm up

1. Work out the answers to these calculations in your head.

    a) 18 621 + 10 000 = ...   b) 6284 + 5000 = ...

    1 mark

2. Work out the answers to these calculations in your head.

    a) 3562 – 2001 = ...   b) 8433 – 3001 = ...

    c) 4417 – 2999 = ...   d) 6076 – 1999 = ...

    2 marks

3. What is 64 881 + 16 021?

$$\begin{array}{r} 6\ 4\ 8\ 8\ 1 \\ +\ 1\ 6\ 0\ 2\ 1 \\ \hline \\ \end{array}$$

....

1 mark

4. A museum had 4462 visitors one day and 4156 visitors the next day.
    They could pick an exhibition on Ancient Rome or on the Mongols.

    In total, 5035 visitors picked the Ancient Rome exhibition.
    How many picked the Mongol exhibition?

....

2 marks

5. Rhiannon wants to check the answer to 4089 + 1944 = 6033.

What rounded calculation should she use to check that it is roughly correct?

.... + ... = ...

1 mark

6. Work out the answers to these calculations.

```
  3 . 8  1  7          5 . 5  6  3
+ 1 . 3  5  3        + 3 . 2  5  1
___________          ___________

...............      ...............
```

2 marks

7. The birds to the right have stolen the numbers Rob used in a calculation.

In his calculation, Rob added the two largest numbers and then subtracted the smallest number.

What was the answer to Rob's calculation?

....

2 marks

END OF TEST

/ 11

Warm up

1. Work out the answers to these calculations in your head.

    a) 165 237 + 20 000 = ...

    b) 336 048 + 50 000 = ...

    1 mark

2. Fill in the gaps to complete these calculations.

    a) 2468 + ... = 3469   b) 8033 + ... = 8232

    1 mark

3. Emma has worked out the calculation 1250 + 635 = 1885.

    Write down an inverse calculation to show her calculation is correct.

    ....

    1 mark

4. Work out:

    a) 70 502 + 55 163

    ....

    1 mark

    b) 48 346 + 31 283

    ....

    1 mark

5. A car weighs 1597 kg with three passengers inside.
The passengers weigh 55 kg, 82 kg and 61 kg.

How much does the car weigh when it is empty?

.... kg

2 marks

6. Work out the answers to these calculations.

```
  8 . 7  4  5              5 . 6  3  3
– 2 . 1  1  8            – 1 . 7  0  0
___________              ___________

..................       ..................
```

2 marks

7. Eoin is putting together this number grid.

The numbers in each row add up to the totals on the right and the numbers in each column add up to the totals at the bottom.

722		1260
	A	966
1031	1195	

What number should he put in box A?

....

2 marks

END OF TEST

/ 11

(10)

Warm up

1. Work out the answers to these calculations in your head.

   a) 4186 + 2998 = ...   b) 6761 + 2002 = ...

   1 mark

2. Fill in the gaps to complete these calculations.

   a) 71 944 – .... = 31 944

   b) 186 151 – .... = 136 151

   1 mark

---

3. Work out the answers to these calculations.

```
    7 7 6 7 4              8 6 4 7 9
  – 6 4 0 5 3            – 1 3 5 0 6
  ___________            ___________

  ...................    ...................
```

   2 marks

4. A theatre has seats on the balcony and on the
   ground floor. Over two weeks, 5925 people sat
   on the balcony and 8813 sat on the ground floor.

   If 7182 people went to the theatre during the first week,
   how many went during the second week?

   ....   _2 marks_

---

5.   Isa is trying to work out the answer to 3987 + 4961.

Work out an estimate for the answer by rounding
each number to the nearest thousand.

.... ______
1 mark

Is the real answer bigger or smaller than your estimate?

.... ______
1 mark

6.   What is 4.275 + 2.56?

.... ______
1 mark

7.   Virat wins a prize at a village fête. From the tickets below,
he picks the three highest values and wins the total.

£8.25   £15.20   £9.55   £11.75   £6.95

He then spends £21.25 of this on a new football shirt.

How much prize money does Virat have left?

£ .... ______
2 marks

END OF TEST

/ 11

Warm up

1. Work out the answers to these calculations in your head.

   a) 48 338 + 2000 = ...

   b) 79 104 + 3000 = ...

   1 mark

2. Work out the answers to these calculations in your head.

   a) 4563 − 3997 = ...   b) 8148 − 3147 = ...

   c) 9435 − 2004 = ...   d) 7096 − 5091 = ...

   2 marks

3. Latoya worked out the calculation 1562 + 331 = 1893.

   Circle **both** of the inverse calculations
   Latoya could use to check her answer.

   1893 + 331 = 2224   1893 − 331 = 1562   1562 − 331 = 1231

   1893 − 1562 = 331   1231 + 331 = 1562   3455 − 1893 = 1562

   2 marks

4. Work out:

   79 292 − 20 532   48 258 − 1755

   ....

   2 marks

5. Dominic is sorting 2000 flower seeds into four bags.
   He puts 130 seeds in the first bag, 1035 seeds
   in the second and 325 seeds in the third.

   How many seeds does he put in the fourth bag?

....

$\overline{\text{2 marks}}$

6. Anastazja is using this spinner to play a game.
   Her first two spins are 1234 and 4119.
   Her final spin is covered up by the star,
   and gives her a winning total of 8888.

   What is Anastazja's final spin?

....

$\overline{\text{2 marks}}$

END OF TEST

/ 11

Test 11

1. Fill in the gaps to complete these calculations.

   a) .... + 3999 = 8156   b) .... + 2001 = 4577

   c) .... + 6002 = 8413   d) .... + 1998 = 9115

   2 marks

2. Work out the answers to these calculations in your head.

   a) 14 811 − 1811 = ...   b) 8187 − 3182 = ...

   1 mark

3. Work out:

   46 151 + 19 493   38 834 + 7262

   ....   *2 marks*

4. Two postmen, Tim and Daud, delivered the same total number
   of items one day. Tim delivered 1056 letters and 525 parcels.

   If Daud delivered 949 letters, how many parcels did he deliver?

   ....   *2 marks*

5. Work out:

5.793 – 1.316

.... <u>1 mark</u>

9.38 – 6.158

.... <u>1 mark</u>

6. Prue wants to do a 50 km bike ride.
These signs show distances between towns.

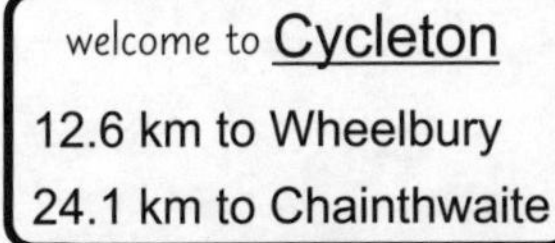

She starts in Cycleton, rides to Wheelbury, then to
Chainthwaite, before riding straight back to Cycleton.

How much longer is this than she would like her ride to be?

.... km <u>2 marks</u>

END OF TEST

/ 11

Warm up

1. Work out the answers to these calculations.

    a) 186 411 + 20 000 = ...

    b) 549 063 + 80 000 = ...

____
1 mark

2. Fill in the gaps to complete these calculations.

    a) 384 705 − .... = 314 705

    b) .... − 60 000 = 630 181

____
1 mark

3. Work out an estimate for the answer to 8941 − 3179.

.... _______
1 mark

4. Work out:

69 335 − 36 148   87 261 − 2347

.... _______
2 marks

5. Carys is pouring water into four bottles. She pours 488 ml into
the first bottle, 612 ml into the second and 500 ml into the third.
She pours 85 ml less into the fourth bottle than the third.

.... ml

2 marks

6. Work out:

6.962 − 2.796   3.831 − 3.27

....

2 marks

7. Some athletes' tops are shown to the right.
George adds up the numbers on the shirts
for each shirt colour.

What is the difference between the totals
he finds for the grey and the white shirts?

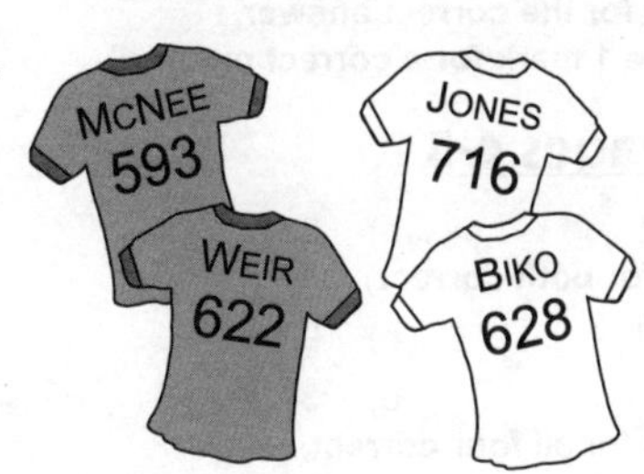

....

2 marks

END OF TEST

/ 11

Answers

Test 1 – pages 2-3

1. a) 2339   b) 5082
   (**1 mark for both correct**)

2. a) 3422   b) 4506
   c) 1715   d) 7189
   (**2 marks for all four correct,
   otherwise 1 mark for at least two correct**)

3.
```
   8 2 1 0        5 3 1 5
 + 1 5 8 2      + 3 1 4 2
 ---------      ---------
   9 7 9 2        8 4 5 7
```
   (**1 mark for each correct answer**)

4.
```
| 54 + 18 = 72 |  | 54 − 18 = 36 |  | 154 − 118 = 36 |

| 36 + 118 = 154 |  | 72 − 18 = 54 |  | 36 + 18 = 54 |
```
   (**2 marks for all three lines correct, otherwise
   1 mark for at least one line correct**)

5.
```
   7.3 9          9.7 3
 − 3.2 6        − 4.4 1
 -------        -------
   4.1 3          5.3 2
```
   (**1 mark for each correct answer**)

6. Tessa spends £1.75 + £2.15:
```
   1.7 5
 + 2.1 5
 -------
   3.9 0
     1
```
   Count up to find how much change she gets from £10:
   10p more than £3.90 is £4. Add £6 to get to £10.
   So her change will be £6.10.
   (**2 marks for the correct answer,
   otherwise 1 mark for a correct method**)

Test 2 – pages 4-5

1. a) 3781   b) 8043
   (**1 mark for both correct**)

2. a) 2678   b) 9255
   c) 8111   d) 3424
   (**2 marks for all four correct,
   otherwise 1 mark for at least two correct**)

3.
```
   4 7 3 8        6 8 3 5
 + 1 4 1 1      +   9 1 4
 ---------      ---------
   6 1 4 9        7 7 4 9
     1              1
```
   (**1 mark for each correct answer**)

4.
```
   7 2 5 7        6 4 2 6
 − 4 2 1 4      − 5 2 1 1
 ---------      ---------
   3 0 4 3        1 2 1 5
```
   (**1 mark for each correct answer**)

5.
```
   5.5 2          9.8 0
 − 2.4 7        − 2.2 3
 -------        -------
   3.0 5          7.5 7
```
   (**1 mark for each correct answer**)

6. Try a few calculations:
   1236 + 250 = 1486, 1436 + 250 = 1686,
   1886 − 400 = 1486, 1436 − 250 = 1186
   There's a match, with an answer of 1486.
   So the only number not used is 1436.
   (**2 marks for the correct answer, otherwise
   1 mark for finding one calculation correctly**)

Test 3 – pages 6-7

1. a) 3158 − 6 = 3152   b) 8245 − 20 = 8225
   c) 1891 − 40 = 1851   d) 4045 − 6 = 4039
   (**2 marks for all four correct,
   otherwise 1 mark for at least two correct**)

2. 113 − 45 and 113 − 68 circled.
   (**1 mark for both calculations circled**)

3.
```
   9 2 1 9        3 7 7 5
 + 4 2 0 3      + 1 8 6 9
 ---------      ---------
 1 3 4 2 2        5 6 4 4
       1          1 1 1
```
   (**1 mark for each correct answer**)

4. First, work out how many cars the factory made.
   Then subtract the number of red cars:
```
   2 1 5 0        3 8 0 0
 + 1 6 5 0      − 2 3 2 0
 ---------      ---------
   3 8 0 0        1 4 8 0
       1
```
   So 1480 of the cars were blue.
   (**2 marks for the correct answer,
   otherwise 1 mark for a correct method**)

5.
```
   6 5 8 9        9 9 5 6
 − 5 8 3 6      −   4 4 8
 ---------      ---------
     7 5 3        9 5 0 8
```
   (**1 mark for each correct answer**)

6. Start with the three rectangles at the top.
   1839 is the sum of 748 and A, so A = 1839 − 748:
```
   1 8 3 9
 −   7 4 8
 ---------
   1 0 9 1
```
   So A = 1091. (**1 mark**)

   Then look at the three rectangles in the
   lower right. A has to be equal to the sum
   of 612 and B, so B = A − 612 = 1091 − 612:
```
   1 0 9 1
 −   6 1 2
 ---------
     4 7 9
```
   So B = 479.
   (**1 mark — also award the mark if the calculation
   is correct but uses an incorrect value for A**)

Test 4 – pages 8-9

1. a) 2371   b) 1642   c) 4173   d) 7334
    (**2 marks for all four correct,**
    otherwise 1 mark for at least two correct)

2. a) 2548 + 200 = 2748
    b) 9115 + 30 = 9145
    (**1 mark for both correct**)

3.
```
  7 1
 8 7 1 7          3 5 6 8
- 2 9 1 2        -   3 7 5
 5 8 0 5          3 1 9 3
```
(**1 mark for each correct answer**)

4. 512 + 294 ≈ 500 + 300 = 800   (**1 mark**)
    3201 − 1933 ≈ 3000 − 2000 = 1000   (**1 mark**)

5.
```
  6.6 2           5.3 4
+ 2.4 5         + 3.2 9
  9.0 7           8.6 3
    1               1
```
(**1 mark for each correct answer**)

6. Start by adding up the weights of everything
    he put in his backpack. Then subtract this from
    the weight of the full backpack:
```
  1.0 5           4.9 5
  2.4 0         - 4.1 7
+ 0.7 2           0.7 8
  4.1 7
    1
```
    So his backpack weighed 0.78 kg when empty.
    (**2 marks for the correct answer,**
    otherwise 1 mark for a correct method)

Test 5 – pages 10-11

1. 184 + 394 and 578 − 184
    (**1 mark for both circled**)

2. a) 9092   b) 1064   c) 8491   d) 4945
    (**2 marks for all four correct,**
    otherwise 1 mark for at least two correct)

3.
```
  9 6 4 4          2 0 5 9
+ 7 1 1 6        +   7 5 4
1 6 7 6 0          2 8 1 3
      1              1 1
```
(**1 mark for each correct answer**)

4. Add up the number of tea bags they use on Monday
    and Tuesday. Then subtract from the total in the box:
```
  4 1 2           1 0 4 0
+ 3 9 5         -   8 0 7
  8 0 7           2 3 3
    1
```
    So the café has 233 tea bags left.
    (**2 marks for the correct answer,**
    otherwise 1 mark for a correct method)

5.
```
  8.2 3           5.1 2
- 4.0 5         - 2.8 0
  4.1 8           2.3 2
```
(**1 mark for each correct answer**)

6. Joe was 2.44 seconds slower than Alice,
    so add this to her time:
```
  1 0.2 5
+    2.4 4
  1 2.6 9
```
    So Joe's time was 12.69 seconds. Hugh was 1.72
    seconds faster than this, so subtract 1.72:
```
  1 2.6 9
-    1.7 2
  1 0.9 7
```
    So Hugh's time was 10.97 seconds.
    (**2 marks for the correct answer,**
    otherwise 1 mark for a correct method)

Test 6 – pages 12-13

1. a) 715   b) 668   c) 658   d) 834
    (**2 marks for all four correct,**
    otherwise 1 mark for at least two correct)

2. a) 204   b) 485   (**1 mark for both correct**)

3.
```
  9 7 0 2          6 2 6 1
- 2 8 6 6        -   8 1 9
  6 8 3 6          5 4 4 2
```
(**1 mark for each correct answer**)

4. 924 − 189 ≈ 900 − 200 = 700
    321 + 287 ≈ 300 + 300 = 600
    694 + 113 ≈ 700 + 100 = 800

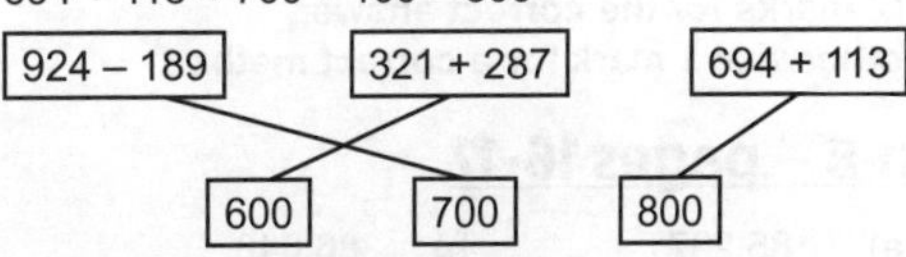

    (**2 marks for all three lines correct,**
    otherwise 1 mark for at least 1 line correct)

5.
```
  9.3 3           4.2 4
- 3.7 9         - 2.6 7
  5.5 4           1.5 7
```
(**1 mark for each correct answer**)

6. The piece moves forward 81 cm, then back 33:
    81 − 33 = 48. Then it moves forward 75:
    48 + 75 = 123, so it's 123 cm from the start.
    The finish is 175 cm from the start so subtract to find
    the answer:
```
  1 7 5
- 1 2 3
    5 2
```
    So the piece is 52 cm from the finish line.
    (**2 marks for the correct answer,**
    otherwise 1 mark for a correct method)

Test 7 – pages 14-15

1. a) 28 621   b) 11 284   (**1 mark for both correct**)

2. a) 1561   b) 5432   c) 1418   d) 4077
    (**2 marks for all four correct,**
    otherwise 1 mark for at least two correct)

Answers

3.
```
    6 4 8 8 1
  + 1 6 0 2 1
    8 0 9 0 2   (1 mark)
    1   1
```

4. Start by working out the total number of visitors.
    Then subtract the number who picked the Ancient
    Rome exhibition:
```
    4 4 6 2        8 6 1 8
  + 4 1 5 6      − 5 0 3 5
    8 6 1 8        3 5 8 3
        1
```
    So 3583 visitors picked the Mongol exhibition.
    (2 marks for the correct answer,
    otherwise 1 mark for a correct method)

5. 4000 + 2000 = 6000 (1 mark)

6.
```
    3.8 1 7          5.5 6 3
  + 1.3 5 3        + 3.2 5 1
    5.1 7 0          8.8 1 4
    1   1                1
```
    (1 mark for each correct answer)

7. The two largest numbers are 6871 and 2180,
    so Rob added these together.
    He then subtracted 737, the smallest number:
```
    6 8 7 1        9 0 5 1
  + 2 1 8 0      − 1 7 3 7
    9 0 5 1        7 3 1 4
    1   1
```
    So his answer was 7314.
    (2 marks for the correct answer,
    otherwise 1 mark for a correct method)

Test 8 – pages 16-17

1. a)   185 237   b)   386 048
    (1 mark for both correct)

2. a)   2468 + 1001 = 3469
    b)   8033 + 199 = 8232
    (1 mark for both correct)

3. 1885 − 635 = 1250 or 1885 − 1250 = 635
    (1 mark for a correct inverse calculation)

4. a)
```
      7 0 5 0 2      b)      4 8 3 4 6
    + 5 5 1 6 3            + 3 1 2 8 3
    1 2 5 6 6 5              7 9 6 2 9
                                    1
```
    (1 mark for each correct answer)

5. Start by adding up the passengers' weights.
    Then subtract this from the weight of the full car:
```
    5 5
    8 2            1 5 9 7
  + 6 1          −   1 9 8
    1 9 8          1 3 9 9
```
    So the car weighs 1399 kg when it is empty.
    (2 marks for the correct answer,
    otherwise 1 mark for a correct method)

6.
```
    8.7 4 5          5.6 3 3
  − 2.1 1 8        − 1.7 0 0
    6.6 2 7          3.9 3 3
```
    (1 mark for each correct answer)

7. You can start with either of the blank boxes.
    E.g. The number in the upper-right box adds to 722
    to give 1260, so it is equal to 1260 − 722:
```
    1 2 6 0
  −   7 2 2
      5 3 8
```
    This number must add to A to give 1195, so A is equal
    to 1195 − 538:
```
    1 1 9 5
  −   5 3 8
      6 5 7
```
    So 657 should go in box A.
    (2 marks for the correct answer,
    otherwise 1 mark for a correct method)

Test 9 – pages 18-19

1. a)   7184   b)   8763
    (1 mark for both correct)

2. a)   71 944 − 40 000 = 31 944
    b)   186 151 − 50 000 = 136 151
    (1 mark for both correct)

3.
```
    7 7 6 7 4        8 6 4 7 9
  − 6 4 0 5 3      − 1 3 5 0 6
    1 3 6 2 1        7 2 9 7 3
```
    (1 mark for each correct answer)

4. Start by working out the total number of people who
    went to the theatre. Then subtract the number of
    people who went during the first week:
```
    5 9 2 5        1 4 7 3 8
  + 8 8 1 3      −   7 1 8 2
    1 4 7 3 8        7 5 5 6
        1
```
    So 7556 people went during the second week.
    (2 marks for the correct answer,
    otherwise 1 mark for a correct method)

5. 3987 + 4961 ≈ 4000 + 5000 = 9000 (1 mark)

    Smaller — you rounded both numbers in the
    calculation up to work out the estimate, so the real
    answer is smaller than your estimate. (1 mark)

6.
```
    4.2 7 5
  + 2.5 6 0
    6.8 3 5   (1 mark)
        1
```

7. The three largest amounts are £15.20, £11.75 and
    £9.55. Find the total, then subtract £21.25 from this:
```
    1 5.2 0
    1 1.7 5        3 6.5 0
  +   9.5 5      − 2 1.2 5
    3 6.5 0        1 5.2 5
    1 1 1
```
    So Virat has £15.25 left.
    (2 marks for the correct answer,
    otherwise 1 mark for a correct method)

1. a) 50 338   b) 82 104   (**1 mark for both correct**)
2. a) 566   b) 5001
    c) 7431   d) 2005
    (**2 marks for all four correct,
    otherwise 1 mark for at least two correct**)
3. 1893 – 331 = 1562 and 1893 – 1562 = 331 circled.
    (**1 mark for each correct calculation circled**)
4.
```
   7⁸9¹2 9 2          4⁷8¹2 5 8
 – 2 0 5 3 2        –   1 7 5 5
 ─────────          ─────────
   5 8 7 6 0          4 6 5 0 3
```
    (**1 mark for each correct answer**)
5. Work out the number of seeds he puts in the first
    three bags. Then subtract from the total number of
    seeds:
```
      1 3 0             ¹9¹
      1 0 3 5         ²0̸0̸ 0 0
    +   3 2 5        – 1 4 9 0
    ─────────        ─────────
      1 4 9 0            5 1 0
          1
```
    So he puts 510 seeds in the fourth bag.
    (**2 marks for the correct answer,
    otherwise 1 mark for a correct method**)
6. Work out the total of her first two spins.
    Then subtract from the winning total:
```
      1 2 3 4           8 8 8 8
    + 4 1 1 9         – 5 3 5 3
    ─────────         ─────────
      5 3 5 3           3 5 3 5
          1
```
    So her final spin is 3535.
    (**2 marks for the correct answer,
    otherwise 1 mark for a correct method**)

1. a) 4157 + 3999 = 8156   b) 2576 + 2001 = 4577
    c) 2411 + 6002 = 8413   d) 7117 + 1998 = 9115
    (**2 marks for all four correct,
    otherwise 1 mark for at least two correct**)
2. a) 13 000   b) 5005
    (**1 mark for both correct**)
3.
```
    4 6 1 5 1          3 8 8 3 4
  + 1 9 4 9 3        +   7 2 6 2
  ───────────        ───────────
    6 5 6 4 4          4 6 0 9 6
      1   1              1 1
```
    (**1 mark for each correct answer**)
4. Work out the number of items Tim delivered
    — this is equal to the number Daud delivered.
    Then subtract the number of letters Daud delivered
    from this total:
```
      1 0 5 6          ⁰1̸⁷5̸¹8̸ 1
    +   5 2 5        –     9 4 9
    ─────────        ───────────
      1 5 8 1              6 3 2
          1
```
    So Daud delivered 632 parcels.
    (**2 marks for the correct answer,
    otherwise 1 mark for a correct method**)

5.
```
    5.7⁸9̸¹3            9.3⁷8̸¹0
  – 1.3 1 6         – 6.1 5 8
  ─────────         ─────────
    4.4 7 7           3.2 2 2
```
    (**1 mark for each correct answer**)
6. She rides 12.6 km to Wheelbury, 15.8 km to
    Chainthwaite and then 24.1 km to Cycleton.
    Add these distances together:
```
      1 2.6
      1 5.8
    + 2 4.1
    ───────
      5 2.5
       1 1
```
    So this is 52.5 – 50 = 2.5 km longer
    than she would like her ride to be.
    (**2 marks for the correct answer,
    otherwise 1 mark for a correct method**)

1. a) 206 411   b) 629 063
    (**1 mark for both correct**)
2. a) 384 705 – 70 000 = 314 705
    b) 690 181 – 60 000 = 630 181
    (**1 mark for both correct**)
3. 8941 – 3179 ≈ 9000 – 3000 = 6000 (**1 mark**)
4.
```
   6 9²3̸²3̸¹5          8⁶7¹2⁵8̸¹1
 – 3 6 1 4 8        –     2 3 4 7
 ───────────        ───────────
   3 3 1 8 7          8 4 9 1 4
```
    (**1 mark for each correct answer**)
5. Work out the amount she pours in the first two:
```
      4 8 8
    + 6 1 2
    ───────
    1 1 0 0
     1 1
```
    So she pours 1100 + 500 = 1600 ml into the first three
    bottles. She pours 500 – 85 = 415 ml into the fourth
    bottle, so she pours 1600 + 415 = 2015 ml into the
    four bottles altogether.
    (**2 marks for the correct answer,
    otherwise 1 mark for a correct method**)
6.
```
   6.⁸9̸¹5̸8̸ 2          3.⁷8̸¹3 1
 – 2.7 9 6         – 3.2 7 0
 ─────────         ─────────
   4.1 6 6           0.5 6 1
```
    (**1 mark for each correct answer**)
7. Work out the totals of the grey shirts
    and the white shirts:
```
      5 9 3             7 1 6
    + 6 2 2           + 6 2 8
    ───────           ───────
    1 2 1 5           1 3 4 4
        1                 1
```
    Then subtract these two totals:
```
    1 3³4̸¹4
  – 1 2 1 5
  ─────────
        1 2 9
```
    So the difference between the totals is 129.
    (**2 marks for the correct answer,
    otherwise 1 mark for a correct method**)

Answers

Progress Chart

That's all the tests in the book done — nice one!

Now fill in this table with all of your scores and see how you got on.

	Score
Test 1	
Test 2	
Test 3	
Test 4	
Test 5	
Test 6	
Test 7	
Test 8	
Test 9	
Test 10	
Test 11	
Test 12	

This page may be photocopied

M5ASXP21